# Pelargoniums

Cover photograph:
Zonal pelargonium 'Cramden Red'.

Overleaf: 'Rouletta', an ivy-leaved geranium.
Both photographs by Michael Warren.

# Pelargoniums

A Wisley handbook

Hazel Key

Cassell

The Royal Horticultural Society

Cassell Educational Limited
Artillery House, Artillery Row
London, SW1P 1RT
for the Royal Horticultural Society

First published 1974
New edition, fully revised and reset 1985
            second impression 1986
            third impression  1988

**British Library Cataloguing in Publication Data**

Key, Hazel
  Pelargoniums.
  1. Geraniums
635.9′33216      SB413.G35

ISBN 0-304-31100-6

Line drawings by Peter Mennim and Sue Wickison
Photographs by Bob Corbin, Peter Godwin, Hazel Key, Pat
Johns, Martyn Rix, Harry Smith Collection, Michael Warren
Design by Lynda Smith

Phototypesetting by Franklyn Graphics, Formby
Printed in Hong Kong by Wing King Tong Co. Ltd

# Contents

Above: Regal pelargonium 'Horace Parsons' (see p.48).
Opposite: Zonal pelargonium 'Cheri Improved'.

# Introduction

*Pelargonium* is the botanical name for a group of plants which includes geraniums or zonal pelargoniums, regal pelargoniums, ivy leaf pelargoniums, scented leaf geraniums and miniature geraniums. This group of plants enjoys worldwide popularity although they are not winter hardy in temperate regions. Millions of plants are produced every year to replace those frosted in winter. But during the last thirty years more and more people have obtained greenhouses, and pelargoniums have become even more popular, for with only a minimum of care plants will provide colour and form all the year round. The so-called geraniums are zonal pelargoniums: this fact causes a lot of confusion. Many people correctly think that the geranium is the plant with a zoned leaf and pink or red, single or double flowers most commonly used as a summer bedding plant. They think (incorrectly) that a pelargonium is the pot plant with plain green leaves and clusters of trumpet shaped flowers in a variety of colours and is some relation to the geranium. This plant is a regal

pelargonium. If you wish to shorten the name then 'regal' is the correct form. If you are talking of pelargoniums then you are really talking collectively about some or all of the plants mentioned in the opening lines of this paragraph. The word 'zonal' on its own is another name for geranium and also of course when it is used in conjunction with the group name pelargonium. It is incorrect to use it with the name geranium, i.e. zonal geranium. In the trade and amongst pelargonium enthusiasts 'zonals' and 'regals' are the common terms for these plants. However for the purpose of this book and because geranium is more commonly used we will use this name throughout, and call regals by their full name, regal pelargoniums.

Pelargoniums grown as pot plants for greenhouse, sunroom, conservatory, or house decoration are very attractive and have simple cultural requirements. With correct management it is possible to have blooms all the year round. There are hundreds of cultivars to choose from and the specialist nurseryman is the best source of supply. Such a nursery issues annual catalogues and offers a very good mail order service. Plants can be ordered by name and they will be sent well packed and individually labelled. Specialist nurserymen can offer a far wider choice of plants than those bought in shops and their prices are often a lot cheaper. The Royal Horticultural Society will be only too pleased to give you the names of these nurseries. There is nearly always at least one nursery exhibiting pelargoniums at the regular RHS shows in London, and also at Chelsea.

### An all-year-round hobby

Many people are finding themselves with time on their hands due to early retirement, redundancy or short-time working and have turned to gardening for a hobby to keep themselves occupied. They find they can spend many happy hours with their plants; however as winter approaches everything stops growing and gardening has to be suspended. If you have a greenhouse, however, this need not happen for it is perfectly feasible to keep geraniums growing on and blooming during the winter and also to be able to propagate them as well if you create the right conditions in your greenhouse.

The first requirement is to extend the hours of daylight. The geranium grows and blooms best with a 16-hour day. To achieve this, strip lighting is needed over the benches using one light to a 3 foot width (90 cm). For example a 10 × 8ft (3 × 2.5 m) greenhouse with 3 ft (90 cm) wide side benches would need two 5ft and two 4ft strip lights to give 9ft long strip lighting on each bench. Next install soil cabling with thermostat all over the benches. The benches should first be lined with polystyrene sheets; then lay the soil cabling 4 inches (10 cm) apart and cover with sharp sand to a depth of 4 inches (10 cm) over them. It is always advisable to have electrical installations checked by a professional electrician, to avoid accidents.

Cuttings (see also pp. 17-21) taken in December and placed on a heated bench set at 60°F (15°C) with the strip lighting suspended by chains to 6 inches (15 cm) above the cuttings, will take a month to root. The strip lighting would need to be left on until 10 pm in December.

If you go on to the white meter electricity tariff which gives half price electricity from midnight until 7 am then you would make your extra light time during the night. Your geraniums will not mind! A small fan heater to back up the soil cabling in very cold weather and all side walls insulated with bubble polythene will create a spring climate in your glasshouse in the winter and so you will be able to enjoy growing your plants out of season. To produce geraniums to bloom in winter (see page 50).

If you are a gardener who wants a break through the winter months but still wants his geraniums to be ready and waiting at the end of February when he gets the growing urge again, then you must, in a manner of speaking, put your plants to bed for the winter. First line your greenhouse on the sides with bubble polythene. Then cut all the plants back to about 4 to 6 inches (10–15 cm) high and remove all leaves; do not take any cuttings, wait until the spring for that. Give the plants a good watering in the pots and then let them become almost dry before watering again. As the winter proceeds, the intervals between watering

Cuttings before trimming (left), and after trimming (right).

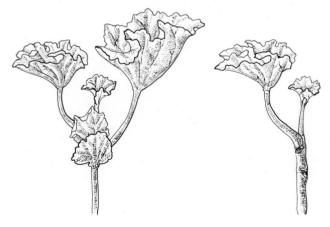

will be longer apart. You only need to put heating on for your plants in the cold weather and if there are only 1 or 2 degrees of frost covering the plants with 2 or 3 thicknesses of newspaper will protect them without using heat. In very severe weather if you are worried about the adequacy of your heating add the newspaper covering as well. It would not matter if the plants were covered for a week, they will survive. Don't water in frosty weather if you have no heat on, wait until the weather improves. Your plants will survive if they are dry. If you cover your plants at night and take the paper off in the day time fix a line up in the greenhouse and hang the paper over it so that it will dry out before putting it back on the plants. By March the danger of really freezing weather is past and in early April you should have shoots on your cut-back plants long enough to be able to take cuttings. During the winter on fine days take the opportunity to ventilate your greenhouse for several hours; it is very beneficial, as it helps to circulate the air without lowering the temperature too much (see also p. 62).

Above: Geraniums make excellent plants for use in window boxes.
Opposite: Some geraniums will grow happily as wall plants.

# Cultivation

## COMPOSTS

Composts for growing all pelargoniums in pots are easily obtainable within the range of ready made potting composts available from gardening retailers. The wide range available, however, does tend to confuse the amateur gardener, the main problems being which compost to use and when to use it.

There are two main groups of compost. One is loam-based and of this the type most often available is John Innes compost. Only compost made up exactly to the John Innes formulae in every respect should bear the label of the John Innes Manufacturers Association – the seal of approval.

The second group is soilless compost, differing from the first group by containing no loam at all. The main basic ingredient is peat, which may be mixed with sand. It is most important to recognise which type of compost you are using. For, although a well-grown plant can be grown with either compost, different methods of potting and growing are needed to produce equal results.

John Innes compost can be obtained in several grades. For pelargonium growing we use John Innes seed compost for seed sowing, John Innes No. 1 for pricking out seedlings or potting up rooted cuttings for the first time, and John Innes No. 2, which is the most suitable for growing plants on through all stages thereafter. The main difference between these three is the amount of fertilizer added, being greater in No. 2 than in No. 1. There is no fertilizer in seed compost. When potting up with J.I. compost firm the plant in the pot. There is no need to feed the plant at all for some weeks and in any case not until the plant shows good root growth around the side of the pot. The fertilizers in this compost are slow acting and long lasting. A plant can grow on for as long as six months with only water and still have enough nourishment.

The most important ingredient in this type of compost is the loam, which should be of the type, texture and quantity as specified in the John Innes formula. Unfortunately, the sources of the right type of loam have become much reduced and this is the reason why soilless composts have been developed.

With a readily available good weed-free medium loam a suitable potting compost can be made up based on the John Innes formula.

Using a gallon bucket as a measure take:

7 buckets of loose medium loam

3 buckets of loose sphagnum peat

2 buckets of coarse lime-free sand or grit.

Spread these ingredients out on a cement floor or wooden board and sprinkle all over 6 oz. (170g) John Innes base fertilizer with $1\frac{1}{2}$ oz. (40g) of ground chalk or limestone. Mix these materials together thoroughly with a spade. Leave the compost for a week before using. Be sure that your bucket measures a gallon. Do not use builders' sand, because the root ball will become too solid and hard after a time.

Growers using soilless compost need to give their plants more attention than they would when using loam-based composts. There are some very good proprietary brands of soilless compost available and good plants can be grown in it but more skill and work is required. However, we must learn how to get the best out of these composts because they are here to stay.

First, in contrast to the loam-based compost, the plant must not be firmed into the pot when potting up because of the high peat content. Just place the compost lightly around the plant and give the pot a tap on the edge of the bench and that is all the firming required.

Immediately water the plant well and leave for a few days. The compost swells and after a week the plant will have firmed up by itself, though be gentle with the watering for a week or so. It is difficult at first to judge when the plant needs water, for the compost can look dry on the top of the pot yet still be quite damp underneath. If you do not realise this it is very easy to overwater in the early stages particularly when potting up cuttings for the first time.

It is just as easy to let the plant get too dry and then it is difficult to get the root ball to take up the water again. Often the only way is to hold the pot down in a bucket of water for a short while until the root ball softens and takes up water.

Another problem with soilless composts is stability. Most gardeners now use plastic pots and when we have a tall, well grown plant which becomes top heavy, it may be difficult to keep it upright. Clay pots would be better because they are heavier, but they are difficult to obtain these days. Using a wider based pot helps a little but if you are growing large plants, particularly for the show bench, clay pots are preferable.

The most important point with a soilless compost, and the one that requires the most skill, is feeding. With these composts feeding is essential almost from the beginning. Because of the structure of the compost the nutrients added to this type of

Above: A mixture of geraniums and lobelia in containers in a cottage garden.
Opposite: Ivy leaf geraniums in an urn at Kelvedon Hall, Essex.

compost are washed out very quickly. The more the pots are watered the quicker the nutrients go, so they will leach out more quickly in the summer when the plants are watered frequently than in the winter when they are watered less. In the summer a plant potted up in a soilless compost will use up all the nutrients in about nine weeks. However, do not wait for this before starting to feed. Some of the nutrients cannot be replaced in the compost once they have gone, so it is better to start topping these up from three weeks after the plant has been potted up. Using a good general proprietary liquid feed, diluted according to the makers' instructions, feed once a week until the plant is potted on into a larger pot; then wait three weeks before starting to feed again at the same rate, continuing until the winter. Once the flower buds appear during the summer change over to high potash tomato feed.

In winter, because the plant is not being watered so often or growing so fast, the nutrients are not being depleted so rapidly or even at a rate that we can gauge accurately. Because of this, it is possible to harm the plant by giving too much nitrogen. Therefore, less feeding is required. It may be needed once every three, four or five weeks during the winter – your eyes must be your guide – but once a week as in summer is too frequent. As soon as the end of the winter comes and the days become lighter, pot the plants on. As spring advances return to weekly feeding.

An easy way out for the winter is to pot the plants into John Innes compost: no feeding is then required and very little watering. However, because we have to have soilless composts we must learn how to handle plants growing in them, especially during the winter. After putting into practice the essential points of winter care, you, as the gardener, must, by using your own judgment, work out the best regime for your conditions taking into account light, heat and rate of growth.

To sum up, using both composts gives the best results. If the rooted cuttings are potted up into a soilless compost they grow away at a faster rate than in a loam-based compost. This is ideal in the early months of the plant's life but when it is getting near flowering then it is time to plant in a loam-based compost. This slows the plant down – the growth is less sappy and the blooms are not so soft and last longer.

After the plant has grown through into the loam-based compost regular high potash feeds (such as tomato fertilizer) will improve flowering performance, though application need not be so frequent or regular as is essential with soilless composts. An occasional omission would not matter; even without feeding at all you will still have a reasonable plant.

## PROPAGATION

Propagation by cuttings is the chief method used for increasing pelargonium stock. As pelargoniums are hybrids of very mixed parentage, vegetative propagation is the only way to reproduce a plant that is the same as its parent. It is quite easy to take cuttings: prepare a mixture in equal portions of damp peat and silver sand or horticultural or Cornish grit. Put this into seed trays or 5-inch (12 cm) pots, water well and then firm.

Take a sharp knife, select a shoot which has three nodes as well as the growing tip and cut the shoot off just above the third node. This will leave the parent plant in a safe condition, for the cut above third node will dry over quickly and this will prevent entry of disease. Trim the cutting back to just below the second joint beneath the growing tip, and remove all leaves and stipules except the immature leaves in the growing tip. The cutting is now ready for insertion. Take a small, blunt-ended, thin cane, make a hole about $\frac{1}{2}$ inch (1 cm) deep, insert the cutting and firm the medium round it. Only cover the bottom joint of the cutting, do not allow the compost to touch or cover the next joint up or rot may start at that joint.

A 5-inch pot will take five or six cuttings for rooting.

A. Cutting established in 3-inch pot and ready for the first stopping; B. Plant with 3 strong shoots and ready for potting on; C. A well-rooted plant after 21 days in a 5-inch pot.

A seed tray will take about fifty cuttings quite comfortably if they are properly stripped. A 5-inch (12 cm) pot should take six cuttings. Place the container of cuttings on the greenhouse bench with bottom heat, if possible of 60°F (16°C) for the first fortnight, reducing by 10°F each week until the temperature is the same as the air temperature. Allow free circulation of air above and around the cuttings. Do not cover them with polythene or use mist spray. Pelargoniums are one of the few plants that must be left uncovered while they are rooting.

Cuttings of geraniums for bedding and regal pelargoniums for pot plants for the following year are usually taken in August or September and at this time of year bottom heat is not necessary. Cuttings can be taken any time from February to October providing the air temperature is about 50°F (10°C). However, if you have bottom heat then in the early months of the year when 50°F air temperature is expensive to maintain the cuttings will be all right with temperature lowered to 40°F (5°C). Even with good bottom heat and ample air temperature cuttings root indifferently during November, December and January because of the short days and poor light conditions. Damping off is likely to be a problem and roots will take a long time to form. It is much better to wait until February when the light is better, and in warm conditions cuttings will root in a month.

Rooting hormone can be used on pelargonium cuttings, but it is not really necessary during the summer though it is helpful in February, March, April, September and October. After the cuttings have been inserted try not to water them for a fortnight, and only water cuttings when they really need it. When watering, try to keep the water off the cuttings, by dribbling the water from the spout of the can between cuttings, or stand the box or pot containing the cuttings in a larger pan containing water; the water level should come three quarters of the way up the outside of the box or pot. Allow the cutting medium to become wet all over by soaking up the water out of the larger pan. This is most important during the autumn and winter, when any drops of water left on the leaves in the cool conditions of winter can encourage the development of fungal rots. Too many losses in cuttings are due to overwatering, the actual cuttings remaining wet in the top. It is the rooting compost that has to be wet and then allowed to nearly dry out before wetting again. When the cuttings are rooted they are potted up into 3-inch (7.5 cm) pots using John Innes No. 2 or a soilless compost. At the same time as potting up, pinch the growing tip out of the plant, so ensuring that it makes its first break low down. This is most important for it results in a well-shaped plant for the future. It is not advisable to pot on cuttings during November, December and January, because of poor light conditions; the plants will not grow away well after the

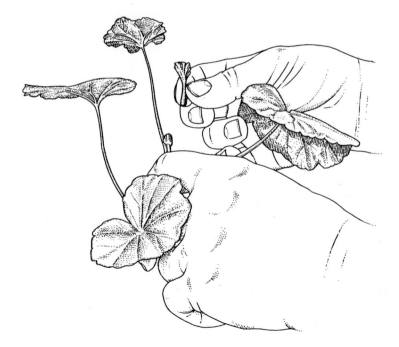

Pinching out the top, or stopping, for the first time (see above).

move. It is better to leave potting up of cuttings until early February. If space is a problem or temperature is not high enough (40°F (5°C) air temperature is needed for these new plants) they can remain in their boxes or pots until April, but then they need to be given a liquid general feed each week starting in January when the growing tip starts to grow away. If the geraniums are to be bedded out they can remain in their 3-inch (7.5 cm) pots until planted out. They can be put into cold frames in April with the lids down and hardened off in May (see p. 29). However if they are intended for growing on as decoration for the greenhouse then they will be potted on into 4-inch (10 cm) pots. If these plants were stopped early, they should have two or three breaks (shoots) and these shoots, if they have two nodes, should have the growing tips removed.

The more a plant is pinched back, the more side shoots will be produced. As each shoot will bear a bloom the plant is then encouraged to flower heavily and also to make a better shape. This procedure is always used to produce specimen show plants: each shoot is stopped at two nodes and any flower buds produced are removed up to six weeks before the show date. After that no more stopping is done and the flowers appear altogether in their first flush in time for the appointed day. The same procedure should be adopted for specimen plants in the greenhouse. Keep pinching until the end of May and then when all the summer bedding plants have gone outside there will be plenty of room to space out your geraniums to give a lovely display all summer. By the end of June it will probably be necessary to pot on again into a $5\frac{1}{2}$ or 6-inch (15 cm) pot; the plant will remain in this pot until the end of the season. Only pot on when the compost is absolutely full of roots. These are the plants to use to produce really large plants next season.

Early in October cut these plants back to about 4 inches (10 cm) and remove all leaves. The plants can be placed close together on the bench or on a shelf above it or even under the bench if the greenhouse has glass right down to the ground. Give an occasional watering to keep the plants just growing on. Early in January they will require potting on into John Innes No. 2 using 8-inch (20 cm) pots. They will have to be handled carefully so as not to knock off any of the little shoots that will be breaking on the stems. The plants now need to be put in full light. As the new shoots grow pinch out the tips as described above. At the same time insert four or five 12-inch (30 cm) green split canes around the plant but at an angle leaning outwards. As the plant grows, the main shoots are tied to these; when the plant reaches full height the canes will be hidden by the foliage. By mid-June you will have

Specimen plants can be overwintered by cutting all stems hard back in autumn (see opposite). In this picture the young new foliage can be seen just starting to appear.

a large handsome plant which will give quality blooms throughout the summer. When the plant starts to flower feed weekly with a high potash liquid feed.

## OVERWINTERING

Keeping pelargoniums for next season through the winter is not difficult, even without a greenhouse or conservatory. Suppose that you have a bed of twenty-four geraniums which you want to flower again next summer. All that is needed is a windowsill inside a room which can accommodate five 5-inch (12 cm) pots and where the temperature remains above freezing even in severe weather. Take cuttings (as described on p. 17) in early August from around the lower part of the geranium plants, so that the display is not spoilt. Using the mixture described on p. 17 insert six cuttings around the outside rim of each pot. This will give thirty cuttings so allowing for a few mishaps. Stand the pots of cuttings in a warm shady part of the garden until mid-September, when they will be rooted. Then bring the pots into the house and place on the windowsill where they are to spend the winter. Water sparingly and only when they become bone dry, which if in an unheated room could be once in fourteen days. From early January start giving a liquid general feed at intervals of not less than a week. If you have the room (e.g. another windowsill) these cuttings can be potted on singly into $2\frac{1}{2}$ or 3-inch (6 cm) pots in February using John Innes No. 1. Do not forget to pinch the growing tip out of each plant when potting on and to keep feeding the plants. If it is not possible to pot the cuttings on they can be left in the 5-inch (12 cm) pots until April. The growing tips will have to be pinched out of the cuttings in February and feeding kept up. In April pot the cuttings into $3\frac{1}{2}$-inch (8 cm) pots in John Innes No. 2 and they can then be put outside into a cold frame or sheltered corner. By the end of May they will be nice bushy plants ready for planting out. The same procedure can be used with regal pelargoniums.

Geranium plants can be dug up out of the garden in the autumn and hung upside down in a frostproof shed, but this method is not very satisfactory and depends a lot on luck. At the end of the winter as the weather gets warmer such plants will be looking brown and decayed but if they are alive will be showing some signs of new growth on the main stem. Cut off all dead shoots and the main stem back to about 4 inches (10 cm). Then pot up these stumps into soilless potting compost for preference, and put them into as much light and warmth as possible. When it is time to bed them out they should be looking more like geraniums again.

There is another method where each plant is rolled up into a tight roll using two double sheets of a large size newspaper. First shake the soil from the roots and make sure the plants are dry. Place all these rolls of plants on top of each other in a wooden box without a lid and store it in a dark frostproof shed or cell. In early spring unwrap them and if they have survived amidst the decaying foliage you will find long pale shoots. These plants are then potted up preferably into soilless compost; all decaying foliage is removed and the elongated shoots shortened by a couple of inches. Place the plants in as much light and warmth as possible and by the end of May they should be looking like healthy geraniums. Of these three methods the taking of cuttings is the most reliable.

## ZONAL PELARGONIUMS WHICH MAKE GOOD SPECIMEN PLANTS

**Always**  Creamy white, flushed pink in centre. Double.
**A. M. Mayne**  Magenta, centre flushed scarlet. Double.
**Baron de Layres**  Pure white. Double.
**Baronne A. de Rothschild**  Pale phlox pink, large flower. Semi double.
**Beauty of El Segundo**  Soft creamy pink. Double.
**Bob Legge**  Bronze zoned leaf. Flesh-pink flowers. Double.
**Brenda Kitson**  Rosy mauve. Semi double.
**Brocade**  Soft red shading to a white centre. Double.
**Burgenland Girl**  Red-pink blooms on a strong compact plant. Semi double.

**Caroline Schmidt**  Cherry red flowers, cream edged leaves. Double.
**Countess Mariza**  Large blooms of soft coral pink. Semi double.
**Cover Girl**  Pale magenta pink. Semi double.
**Decorator**  Bright scarlet, very popular. Semi double.
**Double Jacoby**  Blood red and cherry red. Double.
**Evesham Wonder**  Large blooms of salmon pink, constantly blooming. Semi double.
**Fiat Queen**  Coral salmon. Semi double.
**Glenn Barker**  Shocking pink. Double.
**Hans Rigler**  Red flowers. Semi double.
**Hildegarde**  Orange-red. Semi double.
**Improved Ricard**  Orange scarlet. Semi double.
**King of Denmark**  Porcelain rose, veined and marked geranium lake, vigorous grower. Lighter than 'Queen of Denmark'. Semi double.
**Lief**  Large soft orange-pink blooms. Semi double.
**Lorelei**  Light salmon pink, very attractive. Double.
**Marktbeherrscher**  Rose-carmine with darker markings. Semi double.
**Millie**  Luminous brick red blooms. Semi double.
**Modesty**  Large white blooms, free flowering. Semi double.
**Mrs Lawrence**  Soft pink, suggesting satin. Double.
**Mrs Parker**  Rose-pink double flowers, white edged leaves. Double.
**Noele Gordon**  Pale pink double flowers, bushy habit, prolific flowerer. Double.
**Olympia**  Neon-pink, well formed blooms. Semi double.
**Orange Ricard**  Large orange blooms. Semi double.
**Paul Humphries**  Purple with crimson tinge. Double.
**Queen of Denmark**  Salmon pink. Semi double.
**Radiance**  Coral red, white eye. Double.
**Royal Purple**  Tyrian purple, small white eye. Double.
**Santa Maria**  Large salmon blooms. Semi double.
**Shimmer**  Soft apricot, white centre. Semi double.
**Silberlachs**  Pale pink, compact plant. Semi double.
All the "Irene" cultivars (see p. 24) can also be included in this list.


## OLD ZONAL PELARGONIUM CULTIVARS

The older cultivars of geraniums, many of which were raised during the latter part of the last century and in the early part of this one, are still used a lot, particularly by municipal parks and other public institutions. They still have much to commend them, having stood the test of time. Unfortunately they do not respond at all well to modern growing techniques e.g. soilless composts, automatic watering and feeding. If you are growing or intend to grow any of the cultivars listed below do not use soilless composts, grow them in John Innes No. 2, and beware of over-watering or overfeeding.

Old cultivars are A. M. Mayne, Audrey, Belvedere Glory, Charles Gounod, Dagata, Decorator, Double Jacoby, E. Herbert, Genetrix, Gustav Emich, Hermione, Jean, Jewel, King of Denmark, Lady Ilchester, Mrs Lawrence, Mrs Tarrant, Olympia, Paul Humphries, Pink Raspail, Queen of Denmark, Roscobie,

Royal Purple, Rubella, Ryecroft White, The Speaker, Triomphe de Nancy and the coloured leaf varieties.

The modern cultivars, meaning those introduced since World War 2, fortunately (and this was more by luck than intent) do grow well in soilless composts and can take the continual feeding that goes with it. They can also take most forms of automatic watering though I do not advise overhead misting. These new cultivars do seem to need more water than the old types.

A large number of these newcomers were raised in America and the most well known and useful are a group called "Irenes". These are semi-double cultivars all raised from the original plant which was called 'Irene'. Although they have not quite the clear cut form of the floret that the old semi-doubles have they are superior in every other way. They are the commercial growers' dream for they are easy to grow, give plenty of cuttings, are easy to propagate and produce a saleable plant very quickly. Here is a list of some that are distinctly different from one another:

**Apache**  Darkest of the reds; dark green foliage.
**Better Times**  Soft salmon pink; short jointed plant.
**Cal**  Clear medium salmon flower.
**Corsair**  Light shade of red.
**Dark Red Irene**  Very large bloom of dark red.
**Electra**  Deep neon rose, tinged purple.
**Genie**  Coral red.
**Irene**  Rich crimson; parent of all Irenes.
**Jeweltone**  Deep crimson; short jointed plant.
**La Jolla**  Large, soft crimson blooms.
**Lollipop**  Clear orange scarlet.
**Modesty**  Large white blooms, free flowering.
**Party Dress**  Delicate pale rose-pink blooms.
**Penny**  Fuchsine pink, large white eye.
**Radiant**  Light brick red on short jointed plant.
**Rose Irene**  Rose pink, white eye.
**Toyon**  Sparkling crimson blooms.
**Treasure Chest**  Bright scarlet.
**Warrior**  Medium red shaded salmon.

There is a much longer list of Irenes available but they are so similar to the ones already mentioned that most nurseries have cut down their lists to these basic varieties. If you are growing geraniums for the first time or you want maximum results with minimum of effort then the Irene group is the obvious choice. They will grow well either as pot plants or as garden plants.

# Growing outside in summer

All pelargoniums can be grown outside during the summer but it is mostly geraniums that are used as bedding plants in ever increasing numbers each year. This is because of their ability to

'Polka', a beautiful double zonal pelargonium.

Above: 'Burgenland Girl', a semi double zonal pelargonium, is an excellent specimen plant (see p. 22).
Opposite: A group of double zonal pelargoniums.

flower continuously through the summer and early autumn in all types of weather and situations. During the past decade hybridists all over the world have worked on geraniums with the result that there is today a wide choice. However, when choosing varieties for growing outside the following guide lines may be helpful.

## Choice of flower colour

Red brick walls and red geraniums are all right but in a sombre setting can look a little dull. Try some of the lighter pinks in the same situation and the effect is much lighter and brighter. Put red geraniums against a white or cream wall and the effect is much more startling. Brown or buff coloured bricks are a good background for salmon and coral pinks. A border of mixed geraniums looks brilliant against a green hedge or along a border beside a lawn. The choice of colour is so wide that there must be one that will make your garden look extra special.

## Soil conditions

The fertility of the soil and the moisture content of the planting area should be considered next. Geraniums will grow luxuriously in soil that has been heavily manured but in such a soil they will not flower well. It is better if the soil is a little on the poor side. This cannot always be arranged particularly if the ground has been well fed for a previous crop, so the way to overcome this is to plant the geraniums without removing their pots. This method also helps in a soil that is heavy and damp. Once they have recovered from being planted out geraniums will grow and flower better in a dryish situation. But if the planting position is dry and you do not intend to water your plants then always remove the pots before planting.

## Site

If the planting area receives maximum light for at least two thirds of the day then double or semi-double geraniums can be grown. The advantages of these are that the blooms are larger and longer lasting, and do not shatter in heavy rainstorms. However, in a continuous wet summer the doubles are inclined to hold the damp. The semi-doubles are less trouble in such conditions because the florets are more open. In semi shady areas the singles are best. They are inclined to shatter in heavy storms of rain but in persistently wet seasons they do not hold the damp in the bloom. If the situation is windy, try some of the modern shorter jointed cultivars; they come in all colours and have double, semi-double or single blooms. Geraniums give a poor flowering performance in full shade, so do not attempt to plant there.

## Time of planting

The safe time to start planting geraniums is the last week in May in the south of England, the first week of June in the Midlands and mid-June in the north. Make sure plants are properly hardened off before planting out for in early June there can be some very cold nights. Although the plants will not die if they are chilled their leaves will turn yellow, buds will drop off and they may take until the end of July before recovering.

To harden off geraniums put the plants in cold frames in the first week in May; but prop up the lids in the daytime and shut them down at night. In the second week of May, the lids are lifted

Opposite: A display of pelargoniums at one of the RHS Shows in Vincent Square.

right off in the day and put back on at night and shut down. In the third week in May the lids are taken right off in daytime, put back on at night but propped open unless there is a frost warning. The fourth week in May the lids are off all the time, but kept ready as there may still be a frosty night.

When planting out use a small trowel to make the hole deep enough to take the rootball with about half an inch of soil above it. Plant from 1 to 1½ ft (30–45 cm) apart and the spaces between will soon be filled. During the season keep plants dead-headed to encourage continuous blooming.

## CULTIVARS FOR BEDDING

**Red, single**  Cramden Red, (see cover illustration), Paul Crampel, Prince of Wales, Stadt Bern.
**Red, semi-double**  Decorator, Dark Red Irene, Hans Rigler, Irene Topscore, Toyon.
**Red, double**  Double Jacoby, Paul Humphries, Ruben, Zinc.
**Orange, single**  Maxim Kovalesky.
**Orange, semi-double**  Orange Ricard, Hildegarde.
**Wine Red, double**  A. M. Mayne, Royal Purple, Karl Hagele.
**Pink, single**  Dale Queen, Mme Dubarry, Belvedere Glory.
**Pink, semi-double**  Cal, Genie, King of Denmark, Penny, Rose Irene, Springtime, Hanchen Anders, Rosamunda, Silberlachs.
**White, single**  Snowstorm.
**White, double**  Hermione.
**White, semi-double**  Modesty.
**Coloured leaves**  Caroline Schmidt, Mrs Parker, Flower of Spring, have silver leaves.
Mrs Quilter, the Czar, Macs Red, have bronze zoned leaves.
Crystal Palace Gem, Happy Thought, Mangles Variegated, have butterfly marked leaves of green and yellow.
Mrs Farren, Mrs Pollock, Lass o'Gowrie, have tricolor leaves.

## COLOURED LEAF GERANIUMS

This section of geraniums contains all those that do not have a green leaf with a darker green zone or a plain green leaf. They are as follows – Black leaf, Bronze leaf, Butterfly leaf, Golden leaf, Golden tricolor, Silver leaf and Silver tricolor.

All these have very attractive foliage but the majority of them have small single flowers and when used in bedding schemes (see above) the plants are often kept deflowered. They are quite easy to grow except for the tricolors, which are mainly slow growers. If grown in a too humid atmosphere under glass the leaves lose their

Opposite: 'Cariboo Gold', a fine coloured leaf geranium.

brightness, therefore it is better to grow them in cool dry conditions. These cultivars benefit by being put out into a cold frame as soon as it is possible.

The silver leaf kinds are more vigorous and flower freely. 'Mrs Parker' is rose pink and 'Chelsea Gem' (see p. 35) is pale pink; 'Caroline Schmidt' has a bright cherry red flower. 'Flower of Spring' has a scarlet single flower and 'Hills of Snow' a single pink flower. All of these geraniums are used extensively in massed bedding, for as well as looking very striking they produce cuttings abundantly and root easily.

When coloured leaf geraniums are exhibited on the showbench in the foliage section, the quality and colour of the leaves are the most important points. Therefore it often happens that a smaller harder grown plant of good coloured foliage will win against a larger softer grown plant because the foliage is not of good colour.

The scarlet silver leaf geranium 'Flower of Spring' and mauve ivy leaf 'La France' in a container with petunias.

## IVY LEAF GERANIUMS

These are the trailing geraniums used so much in hanging baskets and window boxes. They have leaves which look like and in some cases smell exactly like *Hedera helix*. They are rather brittle stemmed but the modern short jointed types are easier to handle.

The striking foliage of the coloured leaf geranium 'Miss Burdett-Coutts'.

Most nurserymen grow them tied up to small canes and this is a good idea for the amateur too, for they can be placed closer together on the bench and do not get entangled. Leave in the sticks whilst planting up baskets or window boxes and remove them after the plants have been in their new situation a day or two. If the sticks are removed gently the whole operation can be accomplished without breaking any of the trails. In the early stages stop the growing tips frequently to encourage bushy growth rather than allow the plant to grow away from one tip only. The ivy-leaved geraniums grow quite happily mixed in with other plants but in hanging baskets require a fair amount of moisture. All the best-looking hanging baskets are watered every day. The exception to this is the cultivar with the variegated silver leaf with mauve edges called 'L'Elegante' (see p. 36). This likes extremely dry sunny conditions and for this reason is better grown on its own. In the sunlight and watered once a week the leaves take on a lovely pink colouring. If it is well watered and grown in the shade the pink flush is lost and the leaves become green and white.

Below: A striking example of mixed planting.
Opposite above: 'Chelsea Gem' a silver-leaved geranium (see p. 32).
Opposite below: The ivy leaf geranium 'Mme Crousse' in an urn with lobelia.

'L'Elegante', an ivy-leaved geranium which has a variegated silver leaf with mauve edges (see p.34).

Ivy-leaf geraniums can be grown successfully up a wall in a conservatory. Some support like a piece of trellis should be fixed to the wall from the ground almost to the roof. Choose a bushy plant and plant into the ground or large pot and let the plant grow away, tying up the shoots at intervals all the way up to the top of the roof. They are then allowed to grow downwards unrestrained. Stop the growing tips when they reach halfway on their way back down; this induces them to produce side shoots and by the time they reach the ground you will have a magnificent cascade of bloom. Keep the trails cut off at about 3 or 4 inches (10 cm) from the ground or they will soon become unmanageable. Once the plant is established the falling trails can be cut back to the top of the trellis each autumn so that the plant is kept under control.

## MINIATURE GERANIUMS

Plants in this section of geraniums are less than 8 inches (20 cm) tall with small leaves, single and double flowers in every geranium colour and have green, black, silver or tricolor leaves. They have tremendous flowering potential quite unexpected for their size, and for many gardeners who have space problems, these plants are ideal. They make very good window-sill geraniums for they do not take up too much room or obscure the light.

The number of cultivars in this section has been greatly extended in the past few years especially by the work of English raisers. Black and green leaved cultivars predominate but colour, habit and, most of all, vigour have been bred into them so that the propagating difficulties of some of the older cultivars are things of the past. The tricolor cultivars are the most difficult and very slow growing so that they are not popular commercially and consequently they are not easy to obtain.

Miniatures are best grown in John Innes composts and should be kept on the dry side especially during winter. Do not overpot, by the end of its first year the plant should be in a pot no larger than the 3-inch (7.5 cm) size. Even a three-year old plant should not be in a pot any larger than $4\frac{1}{2}$-inch (11 cm) otherwise it will look out of proportion. If you have an old plant that you wish to keep after its $4\frac{1}{2}$-inch pot is full of roots it is better to repot it back into the same size pot. This is done by shaking all the soil off the roots and trimming them back to about 2 inches (5 cm), then cut back all the stems to about half the size of the plant and repot in fresh John Innes No. 2. Cuttings are best taken during the summer and potted up no later than September.

## SCENTED LEAF GERANIUMS

Strictly speaking these should be called scented leaf pelargoniums because they are more closely related to the regal pelargonium than the geranium having regal type flowers, but common usage decrees that they are scented leaf geraniums. They are fascinating to grow for as well as their many types of scents the foliage grows in such attractive forms. The flowers are rather insignificant in most cases on a small plant, but when large specimen plants bloom then they look very lovely for the whole plant becomes smothered in flower.

The most commonly known is *Pelargonium graveolens* (see p. 42) which due to confusion by the uninitiated is called the oak leaf geranium. The leaf does not look like an oak leaf at all. The true

Above: A group of miniature geraniums (see p. 37).
Opposite above: *Geranium odoratissimum*, one of the prettiest scented leaf geraniums (see p. 41).
Opposite below: *Pelargonium quercifolium*, the oak leaf geranium.

oak leaf geranium looks just like one and is rightly named *P. quercifolium* (see opposite). To cause even further confusion there is a plant with a very nice scented leaf called *P. radula* (see p. 42) which smells of rose-lemon and is used in cooking imparting a flavour like Turkish delight. It looks something like *P. graveolens* only the foliage is cut more finely. These two geraniums have become confused. Consequently when, in a cookery book, the use of oak leaf geranium is suggested for flavouring, it does not mean

*quercifolium* which is not a pleasant flavour, or *graveolens*, but *radula* (see p. 42).

So if you want to order an oak leaf geranium to use in cooking, tell your nurseryman that you want *radula* which is the correct plant. A bunch of leaves swished around in apple jelly just before it is removed from the heat imparts a most delicious flavour. To give a delightful flavour to a sponge, line a cake tin with leaves before the sponge mixture is poured into it and then remove the leaves after the cake is turned out. The leaves of *radula* are even used to make wine though I do not know what it tastes like.

Scented geraniums make very good foliage house plants. They stand up to living room conditions and as well as looking good impart a delightful aroma whenever the leaves are fingered or moved. Their one fault is that they will grow rather large if not kept pinched back. But if they do get too large take the scissors to the plant and cut it down to a more manageable size. It will soon shoot out again.

Here is a list of some of the scented leaf geraniums, suitable as house plants, that look attractive and smell nice:

**Attar of Roses**  Tri-lobed leaves, delicately scented rose, pale purple flowers.

**Citriodorum**  Medium round green leaves, strong citrus scent, pale mauve flowers.

**Clorinda**  Cedar scented tri-lobed leaves, large rose pink flowers.

**Crispum variegatum**  Cream and green curled leaves, lemon scent, mauve flowers.

**Fragrans**  Grey green round leaf, pine scented, white flowers.

**Graveolens**  Orange scented, pink mauve flowers, divided leaf.

**Joy Lucille**  Grey-green divided leaf, peppermint smell, white flower.

**Lady Plymouth**  Cream and green variegated form of *graveolens*, rose scent.

**Mabel Grey**  Rough textured deep cut palmate leaves, very strong citrus smell, purple flowers.

**Odoratissimum**  Grey green round leaves, apple scented, white flowers.

**Prince of Orange**  Orange scented, light green rounded leaves, mauve flowers.

**Quercifolium**  Dark green leaves just like oak leaves, spicy smell, purple flowers.

**Radula**  Straight narrow pointed divided leaves, rose-lemon perfume, mauve flowers.

**Tomentosum**  Large grey-green downy leaves, strong peppermint smell, white flowers (see above).

**Variegated Fragrans**  Green and cream tri-lobular indented leaves, pine scent, white flowers.

Opposite: Two scented leaf geraniums: *Pelargonium graveolens* 'Lady Plymouth' (above), and *Pelargonium radula* (below).

# Regal pelargoniums

The modern regal pelargoniums are bred for their bushy habit, ability to flower all spring and summer as well as their outstanding range of colour and quality of bloom. This has increased their popularity as it is now worth while to use them in ways other than just a windowsill plant or for greenhouse decoration.

Propagation is by the same method as described for geraniums (p. 17). September to October is the best time for taking cuttings in

Opposite above: Regal pelargonium, 'Grand Slam' (see p. 48)
Opposite below: 'Hazel Perfection'.
Below: Regal pelargonium 'Carisbrook'.

order that the plants grow well enough to be in the $4\frac{1}{2}$ or 5-inch (11–12 cm) pot size by April of the following year, when flowering starts. Regals grow faster during the winter than geraniums. The rooted cuttings should be potted up into $2\frac{1}{2}$ or 3-inch (7 cm) pots by the end of November, pinching out the growing tip at the same time. Keep the plants growing on through the winter, they will be quite happy at a temperature of about 40°F (5°C). In February pot into 4 or 5-inch (12 cm) pots of John Innes No. 2 or soilless compost (see p. 13). When the flower buds start to show colour feed weekly with a high potash liquid feed; this helps to maintain a succession of bloom.

Yearling plants should be cut back to about 5 inches (13 cm) in October and watered just enough to keep them growing through the winter until January when they should be potted on into 7 or 8-inch (18–20 cm) pots using John Innes No. 2 compost. These will make very large specimen plants suitable for the showbench or display. Do not forget to feed regularly when flowering begins.

The list of modern regal pelargoniums is prodigious so that any would-be grower of these beautiful plants has a very wide variety

A group of regal pelargoniums including the pink, white and bronze 'Aztec' and mahogany crimson 'Rogue'.

'Dunkery Beacon', a brilliantly coloured regal pelargonium.

of choice. Below is a list of fifty top cultivars and without trying it would be possible to produce another list of fifty and still leave good ones unmentioned.

**Alberts Choice**  Clear orange salmon, slight white throat, compact habit.
**All My Love**  Beautifully marked, orchid mauve or creamy white base.
**Applause**  Pink, white centre, and pearly white frilled edges.
**Ashley Stephenson**  Orange salmon, white throat, compact plant.
**Aztec**  Large flowers of pink, white and bronze shades.
**Beauty of Bath**  Pale mauve and white ruffled flowers.
**Black Magic**  The blackest flower of all black flowers.
**Bredon**  Large wine red flowers, bushy habit.
**Caprice**  Large flowers of rose-red blooms.
**Cezanne**  Upper petals purple, lower petals pale lavender.
**Cherie**  White flowers, maroon mark on each petal.
**Chew Magna**  Pinky white blooms, blotched and veined sienna-red.
**Country Girl**  Soft candy pink, feathered and blotched strawberry.
**Doris Frith**  Creamy white, slightly veined red.
**Dubonnet**  Blush wine red, continuous flowering.
**Dunkery Beacon**  Fiery orange, feathered plum.
**Elgar**  Bright mauve and purple.
**Elsie Hickman**  Pink with white throat, overlaid black and maroon.
**Fascination**  Pale pink, with red and maroon markings.
**Geoffrey Horseman**  Mallow purple blooms with deep purple markings.
**Georgia Peach**  Soft mid-peach pink.

Opposite: Left: 'La Paloma', right: 'Starlight': foreground: 'Rogue'.
Above: The delightful regal pelargonium 'Tip Top Duet' in a
decorative pot.

**Golden Princess**  Variegated green and gold leaf, white flower.

**Grand Slam**  Brilliant combination of crimson and scarlet (see p. 47).

**Hazel**  Large violet purple bloom. Compact habit.

**Horace Parsons**  White bloom with crimson blaze on each petal (see p. 6).

**House and Garden**  Turkey red, maroon top petals, pale mauve-pink throat.

**Jim Field**  Purple black, compact habit.

**Joan Fairman**  White blooms, flushed pink and blotched maroon.

**Joy**  Beautifully frilled, salmon pink blooms with white throat.

**Julie Smith**  Lavender and purple flowers, very pretty.

**Lavender Grand Slam**  Bright lavender purple flowers. Sport of 'Grand Slam'.

**Lowood**  Purple mauve with deep purple markings.

**Marie Rober**  Large violet blooms with darker marks on petals.

**May Magic**  Large open blooms of salmon orange, white throat and edges.

**Mendip**  Large salmon pink flowers, white reverse, top petals flushed vermilion and feathered black.

**Noche**  Maroon red, shading to coral red at edge of petals.

**Pompeii**  Nearly black petals narrowly edged with pinkish white. Compact.

**Purple Emperor**  Large lavender-purple flowers. Late bloomer.

**Quantock**  Salmon pink blooms, with orange flush and purple markings on upper petals.

**Rita Coughlin**  Large flower heads of pale lavender.

**Robbie Hare**  Soft salmon, deepening to orange salmon.

**Rogue**  Huge mahogany crimson flowers, shading to black (see p. 47).

**Sunrise**  Large orange-salmon flowers, with white throat.

**Sybil Bradshaw**  Large wavy blooms of violet lavender.

**Ted Dutton**  Orange-salmon with white throat.

**Victoria Regina**  White with deep purple splashed on each petal.

**Violetta**  Purple with pink centre.

**Wedding Gown**  Pure white large blooms. Slow grower.

**White Glory**  Glistening white flowers, sometimes slightly marked red. Very bushy growth.

# Growing under glass and indoors

## STANDARD PELARGONIUMS

Geraniums and regals will both make very good standards but it takes two years to accomplish this. Cuttings are taken in the normal way and potted on into 3-inch (7 cm) pots; the growing tip is not removed. Plants to be grown as standards should be potted into John Innes No. 2 which is used throughout their life, so giving weight and firmness at the base, enabling the plant to be free standing and remain upright. When the young plant is 6 inches (15 cm) high insert a thin cane 18 inches (45 cm) long into the pot and tie the stem to it in two places, removing side shoots and all leaves except the growing tip. As the plant grows, pot on into a 4-inch (10 cm) pot. Keep tying the stem to the cane at intervals of about 3 inches (7 cm) and continue to remove any leaves and side shoots appearing on the stem taking care not to interfere with the growing tip. When the stem reaches the top of the cane this must be changed for another thicker cane or stake of the height that the standard is to be. The new cane is sharpened at one end and dipped in Cuprinol (allow it to dry thoroughly before inserting). It is best to have some help when changing the canes to avoid breaking the stem which at this stage is rather sappy. Get your helper to hold the stem in two places, at the top and midway down. Meanwhile cut the ties, remove the thin cane, and put the thicker cane in the same hole. Then, quickly re-tie the stem to the cane at the middle, top and bottom, and the rest of the stem can be tied in. When the growing tip reaches two-thirds of the required height, stop removing side shoots and leaves and when it reaches the full height remove the growing tip. After this has been done the side shoots will grow more quickly and these should be stopped at every third joint until a nice round bushy head has been formed. The plant should now be in a 7-inch (18 cm) pot. At the end of the season cut back at each shoot to within three nodes of the main stem. Ties will have to be renewed each year and canes usually every two years. The plant will have to be repotted and when the pot size is getting too large to be handled easily potting down will have to be done as described earlier for

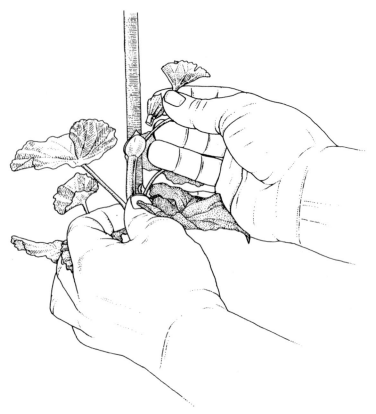

Stopping a standard to form the "head".

miniatures (see p. 37). Standards will grow on for years. I have some plants at least 15 years old and every year they give a lovely display.

## WINTER FLOWERS

Only geraniums will bloom consistently through the winter but they must be grown specially to do this. It is of course necessary to have a heated house with a minimum temperature about 45°F (7°C) for this to be a success. Cuttings are taken and rooted in April, potted up into 3-inch (7 cm) pots. They are stopped and potted on as previously described and by September should be in a 4½-inch (12 cm) pot of John Innes No. 2. During all this time every flower bud must be removed as it forms. From September onwards allow all buds and flowers to develop naturally and feed once a week throughout the winter with a high potash liquid feed. Cultivars that are suitable for winter blooming are listed below:

single ones generally give a better performance than doubles or semi-doubles.

## Singles

**Alberta**  Coral pink and white.
**Beatrix Little**  Intense vermilion, compact habit.
**Belvedere Glory**  Cerise pink.
**Caledonian Maiden**  Rose opal.
**Cramden Red**  Scarlet (see cover illustration).
**Dove**  Mauve.
**Heidi**  Coral red and white.
**Madame Dubarry**  Coral red.
**Paul Gotz**  Short compact habit, scarlet free flowering.
**Prince of Wales**  Crimson blooms, overlaid dark crimson.
**Rachel Fisher**  Deep mauve-pink.
**Snowstorm**  Pure white.
**Vera Dillon**  Light cerise, scarlet centre (see p. 52).
**Willingdon Beauty**  Huge trusses of rosy salmon.

## Doubles

**A.M. Mayne**  Magenta, centre flushed scarlet.
**Double Jacoby**  Blood red and cherry red.
**Pink Raspail**  Fuchsine pink, free flowering.
**Royal Purple**  Tyrian purple, small white eye.

## Semi-doubles

**Dark Red Irene**  Large dark crimson blooms.
**Genie**  Coral red.
**Gustav Emich**  Scarlet bloom.
**Hanchen Anders**  Cerise pink, compact grower.
**Irene**  Crimson blooms.
**Penny**  Fuchsine pink, large white eye.
**Rosamunda**  Coral pink, free flowering, dwarf habit.
**Toyon**  Sparkling crimson blooms.

## GERANIUMS FROM SEED

Until the 1960s geraniums were only raised from seed to produce new cultivars. Any seeds sold were labelled 'mixed varieties'. Due to the complex parentage of geraniums, the number of new worthwhile cultivars produced from a cross is a very small proportion in relation to the numbers of seeds sown. However during the 1960s breeders managed to find a cross which produced identical plants from seed every time the cross was made. This work was done in America, and in California it was possible to get these seed-raised plants to bloom in four months so

A mixture of zonal pelargoniums in a greenhouse.

that it looked as though it was going to be possible to grow geraniums from seed as we do our annual bedding plants. In Britain, however, raising bedding pelargoniums from seed is hampered by the poor light conditions in December and January – the time for sowing. If extra light is provided in the early months as well as high temperature, and a dwarfing regulator such as Cycocel is used it is possible to produce a geranium in flower at the end of May. But the cost of growing a bedding geranium from seed is higher than that of raising them from cuttings. There are now many good strains of geraniums available from seed firms, and they come in many colours, but their flowering performance is not always good outside if they have not been dwarfed in the first year because they are seedling plants, which are always very vigorous and shy of bloom. Cuttings taken from these plants will flower very well without dwarfing. As the flowers are single, they are in no way superior to the tried and tested named varieties already available. Home gardeners in Britain generally seem to prefer double varieties, therefore plants raised from cuttings are still the best for them.

'Apple Blossom Rosebud', one of the noisette geraniums popular with the Victorians for posies and now enjoying a revival.

Some pelargonium specialists offer seed of their own production and this can be quite interesting to grow. It will produce a mixture of types and there are sure to be some plants amongst the seedlings raised that are worth keeping and propagating. Plants from this seed take about ten months to bloom but it is as well to grow the plants as restricted in the root as possible because a seedling given unrestricted root run will make much vegetative growth, without flowering. The quickest way to tell what sort of bloom a seedling is going to produce is to allow the plant to grow 6 to 8 inches (15–20 cm) high and then to take the growing point off as a cutting. This cutting will produce a flower in the summer in about six weeks from rooting so that it is possible to halve the time usually needed to see what flower the seedling plant is going to produce.

When sowing seed use John Innes seed compost and cover the seed with a thin layer of compost or sand. The seed requires a minimum temperature of 55°F (13°C) to germinate and the ideal is 65°F (19°C). Mixed pelargonium seed germinates erratically so that as soon as the seedlings are big enough to handle transplant them into another pan in John Innes No. 1. It is often the seed that takes the longest time to germinate that produces the most interesting pelargonium. Protect the seed from mice when planted, as they will eat every geranium seed in the pan in one night if they are able to get at them! Field mice often take up residence in a glasshouse in the late autumn, and may remain there until early spring without the owner being aware of their presence.

# Pests

*Greenfly* (aphid) is a common pest, but fortunately the easiest to eradicate. Keep an eye open for it early in the year (February). Crimped crinkled leaves are one sign and on the underside of the leaves the aphids will be discovered. If noticed in the early stages it can be kept under control. Spraying with malathion or pirimicarb is most effective.

*Whitefly* is the biggest nuisance because it can now overwinter outside. When the warm weather returns the adults start to breed and in heated greenhouses, they may continue to breed throughout the winter. *Chemicals available for the control of whitefly are resmethrin and bioresmethrin, pyrethrum and HCH. Be prepared to alternate the chemicals used if there is any possibility that pest resistance has built up. Apply the control whilst the infestation is slight for if it really gets a hold it takes some shifting. If you see whitefly flying around you will certainly have it in its two other stages, eggs and larvae, and as we can only get a good kill when it is in the fly stage the chemical being used to kill must be applied at 5-day intervals to kill the adults as they mature and before they start laying eggs. After repeating this treatment 6 times you should eradicate it completely. If you have trouble with this pest every year then the control treatment must be kept up for longer. It is important that whitefly is not allowed to get the upper hand, as it is a most difficult pest to eradicate completely.

If you have a really bad infestation the best thing is to cut the plants back to 4 ins. (10 cm) high, remove any remaining leaves and burn them. As soon as the stems start to shoot, apply the control.

*Caterpillars.* These can be quite a nuisance in July and August and in my experience the caterpillar of the cabbage white butterfly is the worst. It has a definite addiction to geranium leaves. Spray with HCH or trichlorphon at the first signs of trouble or locate the caterpillars and remove them by hand if possible.

*For details of brand names and advice on specific problems write to the Director, RHS Garden, Wisley, Woking, Surrey GU23 6QB.

Greenhouse whitefly on the lower surface of the leaf.

*Sciarid Fly.*  This is also known as the mushroom fly and has become very evident in all glasshouses due to the increased use of soilless composts. The fly is a small black one with oversized transparent wings and is more often to be seen walking rather than flying. The larva is a tiny white worm with a black head and it is this that can do a tremendous amount of damage to geranium cuttings. They attack the base of the cuttings chewing all the roots off and then bore their way into the stems causing blackleg and the collapse of the cutting. On opening a new sealed bag of compost the sciarid fly can be seen crawling around on top of the compost. This is due to the fact that all peat is nowadays dug and left on the side of the bog before being shredded and it is then that the fly gets into the peat, so it is important that when you pot your cuttings or plant up, you also drench the plant with malathion to destroy the grubs which will surely be there.

Control and elimination of both fly and larva must be undertaken. The fly can also be killed by spraying with malathion. When cuttings have been inserted into the rooting medium drench the medium with malathion which will protect them for four weeks.

# Diseases and disorders

*Pelargonium rust.* This is a comparatively new disease affecting geraniums only and it is unfortunately very much on the increase. It must not be ignored if discovered on your plants because it will worsen rapidly. There is no complete cure. The most important thing is always to be on the lookout for rust which usually appears on the undersides of the leaves. It appears as brown powdery rings about a quarter of an inch (6 mm) or less in diameter and as the rings age they show on the upper surface of the leaves as light yellow spots. If you find such rings or spots on just one or two plants then remove these from the greenhouse to deal with them. Wrap the whole plant in a piece of polythene and take it outside. This is to prevent even one spore of the powdery rust floating off and settling on another plant on the way out. Take the package as far away from the greenhouse as possible; then remove the infected leaves, wrap them up in paper and burn at once. Cut the plant down to about 4 inches (10 cm) and remove all remaining foliage. Then dust the stump with zineb dust making sure that all the outer surface of the stem is completely covered. The plant can then be returned to the greenhouse. As a precaution dust all the other plants in the greenhouse with zineb getting as much as possible on the undersides of leaves. More rust may appear on other plants even after this treatment, but immediately it is discovered cut the plant down as already described.

If the rust is not discovered until it has a real hold then the only thing to do is to remove all the leaves and cut the plants back. Dust the stems and as the new shoots appear keep them well covered with zineb dust. This may seem a lot of work for something that is not a certain cure but it is the best that can be done and will stop the infection spreading. Avoid wet humid conditions for your plants and do not water from above, as both of these seem to encourage an attack.

Always examine plants thoroughly when taking cuttings from those growing outside. If they show any signs of rust take the cuttings in the normal way and as far away from your greenhouse as possible. When they are stripped dust them in zineb, they can then be taken into the greenhouse to be planted up. Burn all the leaves removed and the old plants.

Fortunately for us we do have a good chance to control rust because geraniums do not overwinter outside. In countries where

Leaf showing symptoms of pelargonium rust.

geraniums live outside all the year round it is endemic. The rust spore can only live on live leaves so with the winter weather eliminating the danger from outside geraniums it is essential to ensure that the geraniums in our glasshouses do not overwinter with a single spot of rust on their leaves.

We have practised the following procedure for years now and I am convinced that is the reason we keep rust free at our nursery in spite of it being on geraniums in gardens. In early September when we take the autumn cuttings all stock plants are cut down to 4 to 6 inches (10–15 cm) high and every single leaf is removed. All the bare stems are then dusted with zineb dust. (The rose top off the end of a plastic talcum powder container can be removed and the zineb put into the bottle through a paper funnel, push the rose top back on and then squeeze the bottle to puff the powder out*). Any other geraniums that are being kept over until the next season are treated the same way.

All cuttings taken are stripped right down to their immature growing tips and are dusted by placing them about fifty at a time, in a large plastic bag and adding a teaspoon of zineb powder. The top of the bag is secured tightly and then shaken vigorously. The cuttings emerge well covered with dust so that any stray spores will perish. In a matter of weeks the bare stemmed stock plants are shooting all up the stems and by January are ready for us to take cuttings again. A bonus from this seemingly harsh treatment is that we have no problems with botrytis through the winter because all the old foliage is removed, less water is needed and there is better air circulation. We are also able to reduce the overall heat requirement of these plants because the warmth is not required to dry the atmosphere.

This treatment will ensure that your plants are free from rust and you will remain safe until geraniums go out in the garden again. However, your plants can become re-infected by someone else's even if they are some distance away, and they are particularly vulnerable when there is a high wind which will blow the spores onto your plants, even into your greenhouse, as well as in the garden.

Virus diseases. These, as in any plant, are incurable and any infected plants should be destroyed. Those that are virus infected show the signs in the early spring. The young growing leaves at the tip of the plants appear mottled with yellow spots. As the season progresses the spotting may disappear and the leaves become crinkled and distorted. Sometimes with good growing conditions the plants grow out of their virus symptoms but the virus is still in the plants and will reappear next spring. Meanwhile cuttings may have been taken from these diseased plants or sucking insects may have taken the infected sap from them and transferred it to other plants, so that it is essential to destroy any plant that shows signs of virus disease. Plants showing spotting and curling of older leaves at other times of the year should not be assumed to be infected as these signs are also induced by aphids. It is only when the spotting occurs in the young growing tip leaves in March and April that virus should be suspected.

---

*N.B. Always label bottles when they contain weedkiller, fungicide etc. and be sure to keep out of the reach of children.

*Oedema* is a condition caused by the plants taking up too much water causing the cells in the leaves to distend and burst. It often occurs in the ivy leaf geraniums at the end of the winter and early spring. The best cure is to remove the unsightly leaves, stop the growing shoots at every tip and reduce the watering for a week or two.

*Black leg* is caused by fungi and bacteria and attacks chiefly the soft fleshy stems. It thrives in very wet conditions. Newly taken cuttings are vulnerable and if cutting boxes are too wet then the trouble can spread rapidly, especially in the late autumn with widely fluctuating day and night temperatures. These conditions also encourage *Botrytis* which affects the leaves causing them to rot. These two conditions which seem to cause pelargonium growers the greatest problems can now be controlled. Two chemical products for spraying cuttings or plants showing any sign of either of these two diseases have been produced and one is called Benlate. It should be noted, however, that strains of *Botrytis* resistant to its chemical constituent benomyl may build up in the house so that the fungicide will cease to be effective. Use as directed on the packet by the makers.

The other is TCNB sold as smoke cones. These can be used regularly as a precaution through the autumn which I consider the most difficult time for the pelargonium grower. The constant variation in temperature from very high to very low in a period of 24 hours coupled with a damp atmosphere can turn a house of well-grown, green leaved healthy plants overnight into yellow leaved rotting plants with centres of bloom full of wet. The TCNB smokes dry the atmosphere and keeps this botrytis condition under control.

*Leaf yellowing.* This condition can be caused by many things. It is the first visible sign that all is not well. If lower leaves go yellow but remain crisp it is a sign of underwatering. Remove yellow leaves, pinch out growing tips and water plants well making sure the rootball is really soaked; then allow it to dry out before watering again. This is the correct way to water pelargoniums. Watering a little each day especially in hot weather is not good for them.

If lower leaves go yellow and the plant appears to be wilting this is a sign of overwatering. This condition could be fatal; however stop watering for a week and stand the plant up on an inverted pot to enable it to dry out quicker. If at the end of the week there is no sign of blackleg at the base of the stem remove the yellow leaves and pinch out growing tips. Water only when absolutely neces-

Geraniums growing in the nursery.

sary until the stems show signs of new breaks, then take the plant out of the pot, shake off as much soil from the rootball as possible and repot in fresh compost.

If pelargoniums are in a greenhouse heated with a paraffin heater and little or no ventilation is allowed, in less than a week every pelargonium will have yellow leaves, due to the fumes given off by the heater. To prevent this leave a vent open all the time. It need only be open an inch or two. Leave the door of the house wide open for at least an hour each day, weather permitting. Remove all the yellow leaves (they will not turn green again even with correct conditions) and remove the growing tips of small plants, or cut back large plants; this will stimulate them to put out new shoots again quickly.

If you take a pelargonium to a show as a perfect plant and win first prize do not expect to do the same again with the same plant the following week for by then the plant will be showing yellow leaves. Pelargoniums do not like sudden changes of atmosphere and conditions. So, on return from a show remove all buds and flowers and pinch out all growing tips on every shoot. You will be able to show that plant again in six weeks time.

If you receive a parcel of pelargonium plants from a nursery and it has been on the way for longer than four days during hot weather the leaves will be yellowing on arrival. Remove the yellow leaves, pinch out growing tips, pot up and leave the plant in the shade for ten days.

## SOCIETIES

The oldest society for pelargonium enthusiasts is the British Pelargonium and Geranium Society which meets mainly in the London area. The membership secretary is Mrs F. J. Taylor, 23 Beech Crescent, Kidlington, Oxford OX5 1DW. The other main society is the British & European Geranium Society which has other branches and affiliated groups mostly in the Midlands and the North. The secretary of this society is Mr A. Biggin, 'Morval', The Hills, Bradwell, Sheffield S30 2HZ. If you are interested in joining one of these societies write to all the secretaries, see what they have to offer, select the one which will suit you best and join. You will never regret it for whilst you will further your knowledge of the pelargonium you will also make many new friends as well.

The national pelargonium collection is situated at Fibrex Nurseries, Honeybourne Road, Pebworth, near Stratford-upon-Avon, Warwickshire. It is open to visitors at 2 p.m. every day from the second week in June until the last week in September.